Bernard Homer Dixon

The image of the Cross and Lights on the Altar, in the Christian Church, and in heathen temples before the Christian era, especially in the British Isles

together with the history of the triangle, the dove, floral decorations, the easter

egg

Bernard Homer Dixon

The image of the Cross and Lights on the Altar, in the Christian Church, and in heathen temples before the Christian era, especially in the British Isles
together with the history of the triangle, the dove, floral decorations, the easter egg

ISBN/EAN: 9783741190803

Manufactured in Europe, USA, Canada, Australia, Japa

Cover: Foto ©Lupo / pixelio.de

Manufactured and distributed by brebook publishing software (www.brebook.com)

Bernard Homer Dixon

The image of the Cross and Lights on the Altar, in the Christian Church, and in heathen temples before the Christian era, especially in the British Isles

The Image of the Cross.

IN a memoir of the celebrated Bible Commentator, the Rev. Matthew Henry, it is stated that when he was baptized in 1662, by the Rector of Malpas, his father, Philip Henry, requested that the sign of the cross might be dispensed with. It being urged that such an omission was impossible, Philip Henry said to the incumbent : " Then, Sir, let it be at your door !"

Although our English Reformers ordered all crosses, whether carved or painted, to be defaced and destroyed ; for they considered them to be images or likenesses for the use of religion, and therefore contrary to the Second Commandment ; they unfortunately retained the *sign* of the cross in the baptismal service ; but the wisdom of their course was soon doubted, and half a century later it was deemed necessary to explain " The lawful use of the cross in baptism " in the Canons of 1603, and a feebler defence could hardly have been made, for it is therein stated that the name of the cross was reverently esteemed even in the Apostles' time, and the sign was used shortly after, "*for aught that is known to the contrary.*"

If the Convocation knew nothing to the contrary, we cannot plead the same ignorance ; for it is most certain that the cross is the Pagan sign or initial of Tammuz or Bacchus, who is mentioned in Ezekiel (viii. 14): "And behold there sat the women weeping for Tammuz ; " and was not introduced into the Christian Church until long

after the time of the Apostles, who gloried in THE DOC-
TRINE of the cross, and not in the sign or image of what
St. Paul considered an *accursed* tree; in contradiction to
whom Romanists and Ritualists call it a *Holy* tree!

Equally true is it that there is *not the slightest proof
whatever* that our blessed Lord and Saviour suffered on a
cross formed of two sticks crossing each other, for *Stauros,*
a pale fixed upright, a stake, and *Xulon,* a stick, piece of
timber or a tree, are the only words used in the Greek
Testament, and malefactors were often crucified on a
straight post with the hands nailed above the head.

The initial **T** (*tau*), sometimes crossed below the top
like our small *t*, is the same as our T, and was a sacred
symbol of Heathendom long prior to the Christian Era.

In England the Druids made and adored crosses of oak
trees in honour of their Baal, which signifies Lord,
and their lord was Tammuz, who was probably worshipped in Britain long before Ezekiel complained that the
Jewish women had become corrupted and wept for him,
for Timagenes, a Greek historian who flourished about
B. C. 51, is quoted by Ammianus Marcellinus as saying
that the Kelts had a tradition that they were descendants
of the Trojans; and Diodorus Siculus, about B. C. 44,
says, " The Britons lead the life of the ancients, making
use of chariots in battle, such as they say the ancient
heroes used in the Trojan war." Troy was burnt six centuries before the time of Ezekiel.

The river Thames, as well as the Tamar, Tame and
Teme probably received their names from Thammuz or
Tammuz. I have seen other etymons, but am satisfied
with this, which was I think first suggested by Rawlin-
son, especially as it is well known that rivers and foun-
tains were dedicated to the Sun, and Tammuz was the
Sun-god.

Tammuz was fabled to have been slain by a wild boar,
which animal was offered in sacrifice to him. In England

the boar's head soused was anciently the first dish on Christmas Day, and was carried up to the principal table in the hall with great state and solemnity. Wynkin de Worde, in 1521, printed the carol commencing, " The Bore's Heade in hande bring I, with garlands gay and rosemary," as it was sung in his time. The boar's head and this carol are still retained at Oxford, although the reason of the custom is long forgotten ; but can any one doubt that it dates from the time of our Pagan ancestors from whom also we derive the practice of decking our churches and houses with evergreens, and even with mistletoes, that most sacred emblem of the Druids.

At Whiteleaf, in Buckinghamshire, England, is a cross one hundred feet long, cut in the face of the chalk hill in the same manner as the white horses of Wilts and Berks, and which may, therefore, be of as late a date as the time of King Alfred, by whom the two horses are supposed to have been graven, but it is equally probable that they were all the work of the Ancient Britons ; for the horse, or rather a proud-crested mare, was a mystical symbol of Ceredwen, the British Ceres, and is found on the coins of Cunobeline, Boadicea, and others.

In Scotland there are numerous sculptured stones, some of which are elaborately wrought, and decorated frequently with various mystic symbols of constant recurrence, which Wilson says " still remain an enigma to British antiquaries." I trust it will not be considered presumption on my part in offering an explanation of some of them. Many are in all probability pre-Christian, upon which the cross of Tammuz is frequently found combined with serpents, boars, hogs or sows, elephants, lions, fishes, birds, crescents, mirrors like the sign of the planet Venus, and with certain other signs, among them being the peculiar Z symbol, and also the V, one end of which often ends in a " heraldic " lily (of Juno ?). Some

of these are engraved in Wilson's " Prehistoric Scotland "
(London, 1863). On some silver ornaments found at
Norrie's Law, co. Fife, the Z symbol has a fleur-de-lis at
one end, and there is also a cross in a circle, Venus's
looking-glass with a lily handle, and what may have been
intended to represent either the ear of corn of Ceres, or
the thyrsus, or ivy branch, attribute of Bacchus. A few
coins were found with these relics, one of which proved
to be of an Emperor Valentin, the last of whom died
A.D. 455.

The serpent was a symbol of Tammuz as the Serpent-
sun-god; the boar was also sacred to him, the sow was
sacrificed by the Romans to Ceres, and the hog in Scandinavia to Frigga, wife of Odin, and probably also in Scotland to Astarté who was identical with Frigga. The lion
was emblematic in some countries of the Sun, and the
crescent was the well-known emblem of Astarté.

It would be interesting could we discover the meaning
of the fish symbol. Can it have any reference to Dagon,
the well-known Fish-god? One of the names of Bacchus
was Bacchus Ichthys, or " *The fish,*" and the meaning of
the word " Dagon " in Hebrew is " a fish;" and Jerome,
moreover, calls Dagon, *Piscem mœroris*, " The fish of *sor-
row*," which strongly resembles the " Lamented One " or
Bacchus, from the Phœnicean "*bacchos,*" weeping. The two-
horned pontifical mitre is the very mitre of the Dagon of
the Philistines. In profile it is the fish's head with the
mouth open. In Layard's " Babylon and Nineveh "
(p. 343) is an engraving of Dagon, found at Nineveh,
represented as robed in the skin of a fish, the head as
the mitre, the skin on his back and the tail behind his
feet. Perhaps the fish of this monument is intended to
represent the one which Neptune placed among the con-
stellations.

When the early Christians adopted the fish as an emblem of our Blessed Lord it was done in that fatal spirit

of compromise then so common—to make the heathen think
there was but little difference between the two religions.

As regards the birds on these sculptured stones it is
sometimes difficult to distinguish the species, but the dove
is probably among them, as it was also an emblem
of Astarté. Juno means "The Dove," and as Queen of
Heaven Astarté was identical with Juno. The lily which

we too often see preserved in Protestant Churches, in
stained windows, carpets, and the like, was also sacred to
Juno, and is still sacred in the Roman Catholic Church
as the Virgin Mary.

Astarté, who was also the same as Venus, was the consort of Tammuz. She was the Ishtar of Nineveh, the
Isis of Egypt, the Astoreth and Succoth Benoth* of back-

* 2 Kings xvii. 30. This is generally interpreted tents, or booths, but the
preceding verse proves the contrary--"they *made gods* of their own."

sliding Israel, the great Diana of the Ephesians, and the Saxon Eoster, from which is derived our term Easter.

In fact, all the numerous deities of the ancient heathen world were originally the same. In the Orphic Hymns it is expressly so declared, and Porphyry acknowledged that Vesta, Rhea, Ceres, Themis, Priapus, Proserpine, Bacchus, Adonis, Silenus, and the Satyrs were all one and the same, and he is good authority. He was himself a Pagan and a Platonic philosopher who died in Rome in 304. Arnobius tells us that in praying they often said, " Oh, Baal, whether thou be a god or goddess, hear us."

Is the dove in our churches placed there as an emblem of Astarté or Easter, or is it intended as an emblem of that Holy Spirit for sinning against whom such an awful doom is pronounced ? As a religious symbol it is against the laws ecclesiastical and the laws of God, for the Declaration of 1559 expressly forbids the emblem of the *Holy Ghost in the form of a dove,* and the Second Commandment forbids all likenesses or similitudes for religious purposes.

At Meigle, in Scotland, is a cross engraved on a stone, and above each limb is a boar and a hog or sow, evidently the symbols of Tammuz and Astarté, with other figures, (see Frontispiece,) and on the reverse, a fish, serpent, mirror, men and horsemen, and the peculiar Z figure, sometimes styled a sceptre ; and on another stone in the same place is a centaur, bearing in each hand an object, one of which at least appears to be a cross, and under his arm, extending beyond the horse's back, is a branch. This may possibly refer to tree worship, which generally accompanied the sun and serpent worship. At Glammis, is another cross, with a lion above one limb, which was the emblem of the Sun-god under the name of Mithra, opposite to which is a centaur, holding, not the bow, but a battle-axe in each hand. This may have been intended to represent

PRE-CHRISTIAN CROSS AT GLAMMIS, SCOTLAND.

Centaurus himself, who was a son of Apollo, the Sun-god, who was another form of Tammuz.

King Malcolm was murdered at Glammis, according to some histories, and the murderers were drowned in endeavouring to escape; but there are three different accounts of his death. So little are these monuments understood that this cross is called King Malcolm's grave-stone, while in the "Statistical Account of Scotland" (Vol. IX.) it is said that the lion and centaur are supposed to represent the shocking barbarity of the crime, and the fish on the reverse to be symbolical of the lake in which the murderers were drowned. Fish, however, frequently occur on these stones, in connection with which it may be added that Dio and Herodian expressly state that the Caledonians did not eat fish!* There is another cross near Glammis also associated by tradition with King Malcolm, but upon it are two small animals, apparently fawns, and two long-tailed animals, probably panthers, and if so, it is evidently a Pagan cross, for the spotted fawn (*nebros*) was a symbol of Bacchus as representing Nebrod or Nimrod himself, and upon certain occasions in the mystical celebrations, the fawn was torn to pieces in imitation of the sufferings of Bacchus or Osiris. The panther was also sacred to Bacchus, because on one of his expeditions he was covered with a skin of that beast.

There are similar sculptured stones in the Isle of Man of as late a date as the eleventh century, accompanied by Runic inscriptions. That most of the Scotch stones have none tends to prove their earlier origin, as the Druids

---

* Had it been said that the two men in the cauldron (see plate) were symbolical of the drowning it would not have been surprising. Perhaps this scene gave rise to the tradition. Strange pictures abound on these stones, animals devouring each other, men devoured by animals, hunting scenes, nondescript monsters, and even human forms with animal heads, reminding one of the Egyptian divinities. A man tearing open the jaws of a rampant lion (Wilson, vol. ii. p. 235) bears a resemblance to the Assyrian Hercules wrestling with a lion, from a Lycian monument engraved in Layard's Nineveh, for although the Scotch Hercules is armed with a sword, he does not use the weapon.

either absolutely forbade the use of letters, or at least considered them unlawful in matters of religion, and they had therefore wonderful memories, for their youth were obliged to learn and repeat a vast number of lines, some say as many as 20,000 at a time, and were willing to remain under tuition as much as twenty years.

Among the many ancient stone crosses, it is often impossible to distinguish the Pagan from the Christian, for the Christians appear to have continued to employ the same tracery, and sometimes even the same ornaments and symbols. One Scotch cross bears upon it a a man and woman, with a tree between them, which might be taken for a *Christian* representation of Adam and Eve; but there is a similar sculpture in the temple of Osiris at Phylœ, which is beyond doubt, an *Egyptian* delineation of the same subject.

It has been supposed that the crosses of Iona, originally 360 in number, are Pagan, and it is by no means improbable, as Iona was a sacred isle of the Druids before the arrival of Columba. The number, which seems to refer to the revolution of the sun, is given in a MS. of the year 1693, and may be derived from a traditionary account of the number in the time of the Druids, after whom the isle is still sometimes called *Innis nan Druidhneach* (Isle of the Druids). There were, however, many crosses of later date, and one still preserved bears upon it the year 1489.

At Callernish, in the Lewis, is a cruciform Druidical temple (see plate), and there is a cruciform structure near Culloden, generally called five cairns, but Wilson says it may be more accurately described as one gigantic cruciform cairn. There is also a work of the same shape in Ireland, at New Grange, another at Dowth, and Wayland Smith's cave in Berkshire, England, is likewise cruciform. Two of the principal pagodas in India, viz., those of Benares and Mathura are also built in the form of a cross.

DRUIDICAL CRUCIFORM TEMPLE.

Three-armed cruciform cromlechs (**T**) are common in Denmark.

In the Scotch Highlands, a fiery cross was used from time immemorial to as late as the rising of 1745, to call the clans together in time of war. It was a cross of wood, the extremities of which were seared in fire, and extinguished in the blood of a goat, which was killed by the chief himself, with his own sword, and the cross was then sent throughout the country with the utmost celerity.

This fiery cross was called *cran-tara* and *crois-tara*; supposed to signify the tree or cross of shame (*tair*), in allusion to the baseness of those who neglected to join the banner of their chief. It seems to me, however, far more likely that the original signification has been forgotten, and that it must have been the cross of Taran or Thoran, the god of Thunder, who was identical with the Scandinavian Thor, whose weapon was a fylfot cross, the same as the Sanscrit *suastika*, which from the remotest times, was one of the most sacred of the Aryan symbols. Thor's weapon was called his hammer, and was a fiery cross because it denoted the lightning, and from its constantly emitting flashes could only be grasped by a steel glove. Thor's symbols of his hammer, glove and magic girdle are often found on pre-Christian monuments in Scandinavia. It must be noted, moreover, that the goat was sacred to Bacchus, and as the car of Thor was drawn by two goats, it was presumably also sacred to Thor, and in Scotland to Taran, and if so, the killing of the animal with so much ceremony, by the chief himself, with his own sword, was originally, in all probability, intended as a sacrifice to that god.

Schliemann found crosses of various descriptions on Trojan articles. Among them the fylfot or suastika frequently occurred. He says in his " Troy," (London, 1875), that the suastika was a large *fire-machine*, the fire being produced by friction, thus : The cross beams were placed on the ground horizontally, and a piece of wood named Pramantha dropped perpendicularly in a central hole, and worked by a string, produced the *sacred fire*. This fire was a god called Agni, and his mother, the Suastika, was the goddess Maya, Cybele or Venus. From this Praman-

B

tha, the Greeks derived the name and fable of Prometheus who stole the sacred fire from the chariot of the Sun.

The fylfot (many feet) cross, with its bent arms, is very similar to a wheel, and the *Suastika* is probably referred to in the following extract from Shaw's "Moray," (Elgin, 1827). "When a contagious disease enters among cattle, the fire is extinguished in some villages around. Then they force fire *with a wheel*, or by rubbing a piece of dry wood upon another, and therewith burn juniper in the stalls of the cattle, that the smoke may purify the air about them. ....This done, the fires in the houses are re-kindled from the forced fire. All this I have seen done; and it is, no doubt, a Druid custom."

This practice may not yet be entirely obsolete in the County of Elgin, and it would be very interesting could we learn whether the " wheel " was one of four spokes only—a cross in a circle—for if so there could be no doubt of its Druidical origin.

In the Western Isles it required eighty-one married men to make the " sacred fire," nine of whom, by turns, rubbed two planks together, until the fire was produced, and then all the household fires were re-lighted from it. Nine was one of the mystic numbers. The Beltane cakes were ornamented with nine knobs.

In other parts of Scotland this was called *Tein-egin,* or the needfire, and was made by erecting a circular * booth, in which was set a perpendicular post called the augur, provided with four short spokes (a cross), by which it was moved round quickly by as many men as could be collected, until fire was produced.

The Pagan cross was often a perfect wheel; for to identify Tammuz with the Sun, it was frequently inserted in the circle of the Sun. In Egypt, however, the circle was generally at

---

* The sun-temples were generally circular.

the top of the cross, and both gods and mortals were frequently represented as carrying the cross in their hands, holding it by this circle. This cross was called in Latin "*crux ansata*," cross with a handle.

In the *Hunebedden* (Giants' graves), in the Province of Drenthe, Netherlands, round stones of the size of a hen's egg have been found bearing on them crosses in circles.*

The cross in the circle is one of the so-called "ornamental" crosses which Romanists and Romanizers still revere, for they place them in their churches as religious emblems, as emblems of their faith, and they look upon them therefore with reverence; but reverence to an idol is akin to worshipping it.

* Arend. Alg. Geschiedenis des Vaderlands, Amsterdam, 1841.

No writer of the age and the school of the Apostles ever mentions or alludes to any sign, image or form of the Pagan cross, except a certain writer under the assumed name of Barnabas, whose Epistle most critics consider to be the production of an unknown author who published it under the name of the fellow labourer of St. Paul. He is followed by the counterfeit Nicodemus, in the so-called Gospel of Nicodemus. These writers seem to have been half-converted heathens who forged the names of good men to give weight to their crude ideas. Such forgeries were common. Of the fifteen Epistles ascribed to Ignatius, eight are now universally condemned and only three are generally allowed.

Justin Martyr (died about 165) is the first known writer after the Apostles who speaks of the form of the cross, which he evidently takes with other crudities from the hands of the pseudo Barnabas, and half a century later M. Minutius Felix speaks favourably of it, as does also Tertullian who died A.D. 225, whose language seems to admit that the sign of the wood of the cross, or a likeness of the cross in wood, was worshipped in the third century, both by Christians and Pagans. The Rev. Mr. Ward ("History of the Cross," London and Philadelphia, 1871) gives their exact words which are too long to quote here and concludes, "Barnabas, Nicodemus and Justin magnify the power of the sign, but give no hint of worshipping the cross; which worship Minutius and Tertullian agree to justify before the heathen. Thus the wonder grew 'with all deceivableness of unrighteousness' till at length all Christendom was enveloped in delusion."

Tertullian, however, at another period bitterly lamented the inconsistency of Christians; and, when blaming them for taking part in the Pagan festivals, says: "Oh, how much more faithful are the heathens to *their* religion, who take special care to adopt no solemnity from the Christians."

According to Cardinal Baronius, Gregory, Bishop of New Cæsarea (A.D. 264), now Kaiseriyeh, in Armenia, set up wooden crosses in certain places, and was the first who commanded them to be adored.

Cyprian, Bishop of Carthage, and a martyr, who was beheaded A.D. 258, shows that the primitive custom was not to mark the baptised with the murderous cross, but with the sign of Christ, X (*chi*, our ch), the initial of Christ and of God. As it is written "Having His own and His Father's Name written on their foreheads," (Rev. xiv. 1, and xxii. 4). Again he says : "They only escape who are born again and signed with the *Sign of Christ—Signo Christi,)*" which is the initial of the owner's name, X (*chi*). This X (*chi*) the first letter of our Lord's title CH-rist, was called *Signum Christi*, or as Cyprian says, "*Christi Signum Signum Dei*—the sign of Christ and of God.

After a time the monogram was invented. It was composed of the X (*chi*) and P (*rho*), answering to our C H R. This is generally called the Constantinian Monogram, and this, *and not a Pagan Cross*, was adopted by the Emperor Constantine, A.D. 312, and is to be seen on his coins, medals and monuments to this very day. In

some specimens the Emperor's head appears in profile
with the *chi-rho* on the side of his helmet, and on others
is his standard, the famous Labarum, on the top of which
is the *chi rho*. Ambrose calls this "the Labarum, that is
the ensign consecrated by the NAME of Christ, *Christi
sacratum nomine.*".

But the testimony of Lactantius is most decisive. He
was the tutor of Constantine's son, and says the Emperor
was warned in a dream to make the celestial sign of God
upon the soldiers' shields. He did so, and with the *trans-
verse letter* **X** (*chi*) circumflecting the head of it, he marks
Christ upon their shields (*"et transversâ **X** literâ summo
capita circumflexo Christum scutis notat"*). This proves
clearly that the sign which Constantine thought he saw
in a dream was the letter **X** (*chi*), the initial of "Christ"
and not the heathen cross. In the Roman Catacombs
there is a distinct allusion to this on a monument to
"Simphonia and her sons" at the head of which are these
words,

> "In hoc vinces*
> X."

There is an epitaph in the Catacombs of the time of
Hadrian (A.D. 117-138), accompanied by the Constantinian
Monogram, but it is supposed (perhaps without sufficient
reason) to have been added by a later hand; and there is
another of the time of Antoninus (A. D. 161), but its
genuineness has also been doubted. The first unques-
tioned date of the *chi-rho*† monogram in the Catacombs is
of the year 331.‡

---

* By this conquer.
† Are we justified in using even the *chi-rho* monogram in churches? Is it
not an emblem for the use of religion, and are there any exceptions to the
Second Commandment? Three symbols have been given us, and are not
they enough? Water, Bread and Wine, are neither images nor likenesses.
‡ A *chi-rho* monogram has been found on pre-Christian monuments and
coins, and is supposed to be an abbreviation for *Chrŏnŏs*, time, a year, or
Chrŭsŏs, gold, gold coin, or *Archon*, ruler, chief magistrate. The *chi* alone

According to the fable, the Empress Helena is said to have dug up the cross, A.D. 327, but her son Constantine, who lived ten years after, makes no mention of it. Eusebius, the ecclesiastical historian, who was then and for twelve years after Bishop of Cæsarea, in Syria, near the scene, although he mentions Helena's pilgrimage, and what she had done for the clearing and adorning of the Holy Places in Jerusalem, says nothing about the discovery, nor is it mentioned by a Gaulish pilgrim, who described Jerusalem seven years after Helena's visit. It is first mentioned by Cyril, who became Bishop of Jerusalem, A.D. 350, and was the first to distribute the wood of the cross, never intimating how or when it was found. After an episcopate of seven years, however, Cyril was found guilty of having robbed the church of precious things, vessels and ornaments, and was deposed in 357.

About the year 400, the X (*chi*) was changed into the Heathen T (*tau*), and the monogram was also altered, the X (*chi*) being withdrawn, and a crossbar added instead to the P (*rho*).

There, is, it is true, an epitaph of Lannus, probably of the year 303, when Diocletian persecuted the Christians, which is accompanied by a cross and a crescent (emblem of Astarté), but if the two *chi rhos* of the times of Hadrian and Antoninus have been doubted, it would appear as if this also requires some explanation. The inscription is, " *Lannus* X P I *Martir hic requiescit. Sub Dioclisiano passus.* E. P. S.;" i.e., Lannus the martyr of Christ rest here. He suffered under Diocletian. As the letters E. P. S. probably signify *Et Posteris Suis*, and for his successors; perhaps the cross and crescent were added by them, for with this exception, the first dated example of the Heathen cross in the Catacombs, does not occur

was the symbol of the god Ham or Khem in Egypt, and as such was exhibited on the breast of his image. A banner resembling the Labarum appears upon the coins of Hippostratus, King of Bactria, B.C. 130. Could this " labarum " have served as a model for the Emperor ?

until A.D. 370. Dean Burgon said in 1861, in his Letters from Rome, " I question whether a cross occurs on any Christian monument of the first four centuries." Since then, however, this one has been found of the year 370.

Hislop says the Pagan symbol seems first to have crept into the Christian Church in Egypt, which was never thoroughly evangelized, and generally into Africa; but Egypt appears to have taken the lead; and the first form of that which is called the *Christian* cross found on *Christian* monuments there is the unequivocal Pagan Tau or Crux Ansata, the Egyptian "Sign of Life." Sir Gardner Wilkinson says, the early Christians of Egypt adopted this Tau in lieu of the cross, which was afterwards substituted for it.

That the sign of Tammuz was a cross is indubitable. The vestal virgins of Pagan Rome wore it suspended from their necklaces, as the nuns do now, and Wilkinson proves that it was already in use in Egypt *as early as the fifteenth century before the Christian era,* and both men and women frequently had a small cross suspended to a necklace or to the collar of their dress; but I repeat it, there is not the slightest proof whatever that our blessed Saviour was executed upon a cross of the same form. He suffered for our sakes the death of a common malefactor; and criminals, as we have seen, were often crucified upon straight posts or pales, with the hands nailed *above the head.* That our Saviour suffered in that way is not a new supposition; for in a work by the learned antiquarian, Joost Lips (Lipsius), published in Louvain in 1605, He is represented as crucified in that manner. It was engraved in

The Rock newspaper last year. Crosses as instruments of punishment were formerly used in marvellous numbers, so that it can hardly be supposed they would be particular about the form of them. Varus crucified 2,000 Jews, Hadrian 500 a day, and Titus so many, "that there was no room for the crosses and no crosses for the bodies."

At the period of the Revolution in England, a Royal Commission, appointed to inquire into the rites and ceremonies of the Church, numbering among its members eight or ten bishops, strongly recommended that the use of the cross in baptism, as tending to superstition, should be laid aside.

When the Prayer Book of the Protestant Episcopal Church in the United States of America was revised in 1789, a rubric was added, permitting the minister to omit making the sign of the cross, if desired. The Reformed Episcopalians went a step further, and according to their Prayer Book (Philadelphia, 1874), the sign is not to be made except when it is desired, but in the Book of the Prayer Book Revision Society (London, 1874), of which Lord Ebury is President, the sign of the cross is entirely omitted.

Strange to say, however, it is retained in the new Prayer Book of the Church of Ireland (Dublin, 1878), although it has therein been deemed necessary not only to print an apologetical note at the end of the Baptismal Service, but also the whole of the Thirtieth Canon of the year 1603. Nevertheless, although they retain the cross in their service, and defend its use there by the old canon, they have dropped from the Calender the "Invention of the Cross" (May 3) and "Holy Cross Day" (Sept. 14). Their own Thirty-sixth Canon is as follows:—"There shall not be any cross on the Communion Table, or on the covering thereof, nor shall a cross be erected or depicted on the wall or other structure behind the Communion Table," and the Thirty-ninth Canon forbids carrying any

cross in processions. The Fifth Canon is, " No minister
or other person during the time of Divine Service shall
make the sign of the Cross *save where prescribed in the
Rubric,*" i.e., in the Baptismal Service! Is this consistent?
and why should the innocent babes alone be branded with
the sign of the accursed tree when it is prohibited everywhere else ?

And why should we still continue to build our churches
in the form of a cross ? It is time to do away with those
deep chancels which Puseyites consider as Holies of
Holies, fit only for "priests and their assistants," the surpliced choir, and not to be desecrated by "unhallowed
feet " (lay feet). Bishop Hooper, the martyr, said:—" I
would wish that the magistrates should *shut up the par-
tition called the chancel* that separateth the congregation
of Christ one from other," and Bucer also (whose bones
were exhumed and burnt by Bloody Mary), inveighed
vehemently against them. At a conference held in Derby,
England, last November (1878), Canon Ryle warned his
hearers to look to their chancels and tables ; and the Rev.
Sholto D. C. Douglas (then a Vicar in Derby, but now
Rector of All Souls, Langham Place, London, where he has
re-introduced the black gown, changed the weekly communion to evening communion twice a month, and applied for a faculty to remove the cross from behind the
table), said that "*chancels were the root of all evil,*" and declared it as his opinion that there should not be any.
Others advocated the removal of the table to the body of
the church (according to the rubric, and as they were
placed during the first six centuries), and the removal of
the organs from the chancels (so that there would be no
danger of having surpliced choirs), and disapproved of
windows with figures.

It is now more than thirty years since Dean Close published his sermon, "The Restoration of Churches is the
Restoration of Popery," and he has proved a true prophet.

I have it before me now,* as well as a critique "Pusey-ite Developments," bought in 1850, at about which time I first began to take particular notice of the proceedings of the Ritualistic Dissenters, as Hely Smith calls them. Too many, as I well remember, considered their innovations as trifles then, and, alas! too many consider them as trifles still.

In Scotland the Reformation was more perfect than in England. Not only was the cross removed from the churches, but the sign was omitted in baptism, and even the hot-cross-bun of Good Friday was abolished! And here, before ejaculating "Absurd," let the reader pause—for the only difference between the English Churchmen of to-day and the Pagans of old, is that while the Churchmen still eat their cross-buns, the Pagans, centuries before Christ, offered them first to Tammuz! These buns which were called in the Greek "boun," were consecrated to Bacchus and were used in his mysteries.† Two were found at Herculaneum, one of which was engraved in "*The Rock*" not long since. There were several kinds of sacred bread, which used to be offered up to the gods, one of which, a thin, round cake now represented by the wafer used in the Romish Mass, was called *Köllyris*, and is the one referred to in Jeremiah (vii. 18), "The women . . . make cakes to the Queen of Heaven," or Astarté."

The heathen cross originated in Babylon and from thence reached to the uttermost parts of the earth, including even the so-called New World, for the Spaniards, to

* I am happy to say the Dean has just allowed his publisher to issue a new edition.

† The reader cannot but notice the frequent repetition of the word "mysteries," which was the essence of the Pagan religion. The term " mystery " is never applied to the sacrament in Holy Writ, and it is, to say the least, unfortunate, that we have it in our Prayer Book, for where, except to a believer in the real presence, is the mystery in the bread and wine? In the Book of the P. B. Revision Society the words "holy mysteries" are altered to "holy ordinance," and in that of the R. E. Church to "Holy Supper."

their surprise, found crosses in Mexico, and moreover, the Mexicans carried them in processions.

Are we any wiser in this nineteenth century:

> " Now a gilt cross on Dora's prayer-book shines,
> As toward the Church her solemn step inclines ;
> Now from her neck one dangles in the dance,
> As if thereby she heavenward claimed advance."

An English evangelist, who was here about three years ago, said he had seen more pictorial and other crosses in the United States of America and Canada than in England, and principally to his surprise in the houses of Methodists ! And yet his visits were confined to Protestants, in name at least.

There are some whose excuse for wearing the image of the cross is, that it is the sign of the Son of man which is to appear at the time of the Second Coming, and others that it is the mark referred to in Ezekiel (ix. 4.), but in the first instance the sign (whatever it may be) is to appear in Heaven, *not on earth*, and it is the sign of our Lord Jesus Christ Himself, *not of sinful man ;* and in the second, the mark (which some believe to be a *tau* cross, but who can surely tell) is to be made by the man appointed for the work, *not by the sinner himself*, who is not to be his own judge. If the sign and the mark are both crosses, as some think, which is it the most likely to be—the cross-shaped letter *chi* (**X**) for Xt., or the accursed tree ?

The floral crosses that hang on so many of our walls, are similar to those of the ancient Manicheans, and to this day a flowery cross is a favourite emblem of the Buddhists. The cross in the hand of Hera, the Assyrian Venus (*vide* Layard's " Nineveh ") appears to have a single leaf issuing from each side. In the Roman Catholic " Office of the Cross " we read, " Hail, O Cross . . . . among the trees there is none like thee, in *leaf, flower* and *bud*," and in " Hymns Ancient and Modern," " *None in foliage, none in blossom, none in fruit,* thy peer may be," and yet St. Paul called it accursed!

Some among us paint wheat ears in the church windows as emblems of the bread, and fill their churches with them at harvest festivals, but are they not emblems of Isis or Ceres, still to be found on medals or coins as classical scholars well know, and do not the Romanists in one of their litanies pray to that very corn, " Bread corn of the elect, have mercy upon us ?" Corn must have been also sacred to Dagon, who was sometimes called the Corngiver (*Dagōn os esti Sitōn*).

The Druids were devoted worshippers of Ceridwen, the British Ceres, and they were celebrated in their mystic poems, as " bearers of the ears of corn."

Here again we perceive early traditions misunderstood, and perverted more and more, as men departed from the truth, and so far was it carried that the Mexicans, who had a deity called Centeotl, the daughter of heaven and goddess of corn, offered children in sacrifice at the first appearance of green corn above the earth !

In Leviticus (ii. 14.) God's people are commanded to offer for their offerings " green ears of corn," but harvest offerings and harvest festivals are needless now, and worse than needless, for they are no pleasure to Him who, nineteen centuries ago, by one offering, once offered, perfected forever them that are sanctified, and the Word to us is "Sacrifice and offering and burnt offerings and offering for sin *Thou wouldest not, neither hadst pleasure therein.*"

The mention of painted windows reminds me that the late Count Krasinski understood perfectly the danger of introducing images and paintings into the church. " It was (he said) replacing intellect by sight. Instead of elevating man towards God, it was bringing down the Deity to the level of his finite intellect." And Ruskin says : " A picture in coloured glass is one of the most vulgar of barbarisms and only fit to be ranked with the gauze transparencies and chemical illuminations of the sensational stage."

And still, so prone are we to see only the mote in our brother's eye, that we all look with scornful pity upon the bigotry of the French Canadians, and upon what occurred in the Province of Quebec not very long since, when in one of the principal cities they set up new gas-lamp posts with the usual *cross*-bar to support the lamp-lighter's ladder (which the old posts did not have), and the *habitants* as they came in from the country thought the towns-people were suddenly becoming exceedingly pious, and stopped and crossed themselves before every lamp-post.

The Second Commandment is the only commandment accompanied by a curse—and it is a most fearful one—but it is accompanied also by a blessing. Shall your children inherit the curse or the blessing ? It depends upon yourselves.

"And the Lord spake unto you . . . . ye heard the voice of the words, *but saw no similitude*. . . . ."

"Take ye therefore good heed unto yourselves ; *for ye saw no manner of similitude* on the day that the Lord spake unto you. . . . ."

"Lest ye corrupt yourselves, and make you a graven image, *the similitude of any figure*. . . . ."

"Take heed unto yourselves, *lest ye forget* the covenant of the Lord your God, which he made with you, and make you a graven image, or *the likeness of anything*, which the Lord thy God hath given thee.

"When thou shalt beget children, and children's children, and ye shall have remained long in the land, and shall corrupt yourselves, and make a graven image, or *the likeness of anything*, and shalt do evil in the sight of the Lord thy God. . . . . I call heaven and earth to witness against you. . . . ."

Lights on the Altar.

THESE are, of course, only to be found in Roman Catholic or Puseyite churches, for no church can be called truly Protestant where there are either lights for ceremonial purposes, or an altar, although it must be confessed in too many Evangelical churches we still see the tables boxed up like sham altars, instead of being "moveable tables, in the ordinary sense of the word," as the Queen's Privy Council decided was the meaning of the Act of the year 1564.

The imitation altars were first introduced in the time of Archbishop Laud, and the laity, although disapproving of them, carelessly allowed them to pass, simply expressing their dislike by styling them "Box Altars." At the same time, too, the priest-party commenced to turn the desks sideways, because, as they said, the priest should face the people when reading or preaching, but when speaking to God, he should turn and face Him. Thus localizing the Deity as if He was not present everywhere, but only to be found on the table, or in one particular corner of the Heavens; and, moreover, making it necessary for travellers to carry compasses!

With the reading desk in its proper position, a lectern is useless, for as a writer in *The Rock* said lately, "What reason is there in moving from one place to another to conduct different parts of the Protestant service of our Church?"

The Jews prayed towards the Temple because the Shekinah was there, but there is no Shekinah on earth now and therefore no Holy of Holies. The Mahommedans turn to Mecca to pray, and in my younger days I often saw my fellow-passengers go to the man at the wheel and by signs or the word " Mecca," ask the proper direction, and it struck me as strange that they never seemed to consider that the sailor, whom they believed to be an infidel, might ruin the effect of their prayers by directing them to the wrong quarter !

The Irish Church have carefully guarded against the use either of altars or sham altars, and against lights in the daytime.

The Canons printed in their new Prayer Book (Dublin, 1878) declare that " The Communion Table shall be a moveable table of wood," and also " There shall not be any lamps or candles on the Communion Table, or in any other part of the church, during, etc.,.except where they are necessary for the purpose of giving light."

Lights on the altar were unknown to the early Christians, and the practice was ridiculed by Lactantius, who died in 330 ; but it crept gradually into the Church, and about the year 400, we find Vigilantius attacking the lighting of candles at the tombs of the saints in the daytime as a pagan superstition.

We are told in the Apocryphal Book of Baruch that the Babylonians lighted up candles to their gods. " They light them candles, yea, more than for themselves, whereof they cannot see one." This was neither more nor less than the worship of Tammuz, the human representative of the Sun, the great Fire-god, and Tammuz moreover was identical with Zoroaster, as is shown by the Rev. Mr. Hislop. (" The Two Babylons," London, 1871).

Tammuz or Thammuz, *i. e.*, the perfecting fire, or fire the perfector, was also known by other names and titles, as Shamash, Shems (and he is worshipped to this day in Asia Minor as Sheick Shems), Nimrod, Dionysus, Mithra, Osiris, Bacchus, Adonis* (from *Adon*, Lord), Odin, Woden (whence our Wodenesdaeg or Wednesday), and in Mexico as Wodan, Baal or Bel (Lord), and other appellations. As a preserver he was called Baal-Chon; as a destroyer Baal-Moloch; as presiding over the decomposition of those destroyed beings whence new life was again to spring Baal-Zebub, or the Lord of the fly, and it also signifies the restless Lord. Worshipped at Tyre he became Baal-Tsur; at Sidon, Baal-Sidon; at Tarsus, Baal-Tars. The Phœnicians adored him as Baal-Samen, Lord of Heaven, and in Ireland he was worshipped under the same name Beuil-Samhan, and the night of the first of November is called in Erse Oidhche Samhna, the night of Samhan, and in Gaelic Samhuinn.

In fact, this God had so many appellations that Sophocles called Bacchus the *many-named*, and the poet probably only knew his classical names. Bacchus was sometimes represented with a head-band of crosses.

---

* Jerome who lived in Palestine when the rites of Tammuz were still observed, in his *Commentary on Ezekiel* expressly identifies Tammuz and Adonis.

C

In Scotland, May-day is called Beltane, or Baal's fire, and in the Isle of Man Boaldyn, and there is a Gaelic proverb, " Eadar da theine Beil "—between the two fires of Baal. In Ireland, May-day is called Lla Beuil-tinne, the the day of Baal's fire, and the rent due on that day is styled Cios-na-Beuil-tinne, the rent of Baal's fire. In Brittany, a Roman Catholic priest is called Belek, servant of Bel.

Numerous local names in the British Isles commence with Bal, and although in most cases this may signify a town or dwelling, still when there are Druidical remains in the neighbourhood many of them must be derived from Baal. Baltimore, for instance, is evidently " Baal-ti-mor," the Great House of Baal.

Tammuz was also worshipped by the Kelto Britons as Gran, Graine, Grein and Grian. The river Cam, in England, was formerly called Grant, Cambridge, Grantabryg and Granchester, Caer Grant, or Grauntsethe. In the West Riding of York is a place called Greenfield, where there are several Druidical remains. At Graned Tor, county Derby, are also symptoms of the same worship, and there are traces of tumuli at Greenford, co. Middlesex.

The Irish Druids called the Zodiac Beach Grian, the Revolution of the Sun, and the Solstices were termed Grian stad, or the Sun's stopping places.

Tory Hill, County Kilkenny, Ireland, is called in Erse, " Sleigh Grian," or the Hill of the Sun. Druidical remains have been found there, and an inscribed stone believed to read, " Beli Duiose," and to signify Bel Dionusos.

In the County of Leitrim there are two cromlechs, called by the common people, " Leaba Dearmud is Graine" —Diarmad and Grian's beds ; and the same name is generally bestowed upon cromlechs in the north and west of Ireland. Here we have an illiterate peasantry preserving the names of two of their ancient gods for fourteen centuries at least; for while the names of places would be preserved in writings, the names of these unimportant stones have probably been handed down by oral tradition. Diarmad is said to have eloped with the wife of Finn Mac Cumhal, or Fingal as he is usually called. Her name was Graine, and the peasantry have connected these monuments with her, possibly because they are styled beds, but the cromlechs in Holland are also called beds or graves (*Hunebedden*), and in Denmark Giant's Chambers.

But it may be asked who is Diarmad? "The Book of the Dean of Lismore" (Scotland) will show. The Dean, who died in 1551, left a MS. volume of poems, one of which is headed, "A houdir so Ossin," The author is Ossian, wherein mention is made of this "dermit doone," in modern Gaelic Diarmad donn; and in a Lament for the Death of Dermit M'O'Zwine (Diarmad Mac O'Duine), by Allan McRorie, in the same collection, occur the words, " *Women all mourn* this sad and piteous tale."

Ossian, the author of the first poem, was living as late as A.D. 432. He says, "I have seen dermit doone," but he may have meant *in a dream*, for in another poem he says, "I saw the household of Finn. . . . I saw by my side a *vision*." Possibly he had then outlived them all.

This Diarmad was the Keltic Adonis. Like Adonis of the Greeks, and Baldur of the Scandinavians, he was celebrated for his beauty.* Apollo was golden-haired, and Diarmad had long yellow locks ; like Adonis, Diarmad was a huntsman, like him and Tammuz, he was slain by a wild boar (and in the case of both Diarmad and Tammuz it was accidental), like Adonis and Tammuz, all the women wept for him, and all the world wept for Baldur, and while the demi-god Achilles was

---

* Diarmad had a *ball-scirce*, or beauty-spot, which no woman could resist, and Baldur was so fair that light was said to emanate from him.

invulnerable except in his heel, Diarmad was invulnerable
except in the sole of his foot, and Baldur was invulnerable against everything—weapons, diseases, poisons, wild
beasts—the mistletoe only excepted, and he was killed
by a twig of mistletoe, or a magic spear made of the
mistletoe. Like Achilles, Diarmad was also a victim of
jealousy. According to the Irish legend of the elopement
of Diarmad and Graine, the fugitives escaped for a year
and a day, during which time they never slept in the same
bed for more than one night. Hence they say there are
366 of these beds in Ireland; an evident allusion to the
revolution of the Sun, and to the Sun-god.

This Keltic Adonis is the fabled ancestor of the Clan
Cambel, or Campbell, who have been known in the Highlands for ages as Siol or Clann Diarmaid, the race, tribe,
or children of Diarmad, and also as Siol or Clann
O'Duine, the Clan O'Duine. They are said in some traditions to have derived their name Cambel from the grace-
fully curved or arched mouth (*cam-beul*) of their great
and beautiful ancestor,* and it was anciently spelt Cambel, appearing first in a charter of the year 1266, and
among the signers of Ragman Roll, before the year 1297,
are seven Cambels, all men of rank.

According to tradition they were lords or petty kings
of Lochow, in the reign of Fergus the Second, who died
A.D. 420. This period was about the most important of
the Irish immigration, although the first arrival of the
Irish Gael in Argyle is said to have taken place in 258.

The prefix O', signifying grandson or descendant, is

---

* Cam signifies curved, bent, crooked, and Cambel is generally defined Wry-
mouth. A tribe descended from the Stewarts of Garth are called Cam-
achas, from a bend or deformity in his leg, by which their ancestor was dis-
tinguished from others of his name. In Lowland Scotch they are called
Cruickshank, but their Clan name is Stuart.

The "Campo Bello" tale is a fiction of the Senachies, concocted at a
time when they prided themselves upon finding Norman origins for all the
great families. Diarmad, however, is a hero of history and mythology
both, and it is not always clear where to draw the line.

peculiar to Ireland, while Mac, or son, is common to both countries. The two combined is, however, uncommon. In McRorie's poem of only fifty-two lines, dermit is also written yermit and zermit, and M ' O ' Zwyne occurs also as M'Ozwnn, M'ozunn, Makozunn, M'ezoynn, M'czwnn, and V'czwn.*

In Fingal, as translated by Macpherson, he is called Dermid of the dark brown hair, but in his case the " donn" probably signified dark complexioned, for McRorie calls him yellow haired, and I think there are no less than three places in Scotland where he is said to have died by a wound in his foot from the *bristle* of a wild boar, while Tammuz was killed by the *tusk* of a boar.

According to an ancient bard, Fingal's banner had inscribed upon it " *Dealbh Ghrcine*," the image of the Sun. Logan says, " This was much respected as the King's ensign, but the flag of Diarmad, who led the right wing of the army, seems to have been superior." This flag, the same bard calls the " Lia Luinneach."

It would be a subject full of interest, could we ascertain how long the clan have borne the two names of Children of Diarmad or Adonis, and Cambel. As a tribe they may have been in existence long prior to these dates, and the tradition that they came from Ireland is undoubtedly a true one. A leader of the Gauls, B.C. 279, was named Cambaul (*Cambaules*). Could that have been even then a clan name ? It is not a very wild suggestion to hint at such a source, for there must have been considerable intercourse between Ireland and Gaul, as so intimate were the relations between England and the mainland, that Cæsar, 56 years before our Saviour's birth, tells us the Gauls were accustomed to send their children to England for their education, and Tacitus says that the language of the Gauls and Britons was identical.

---

* There are many interchangeable letters in the Keltic tongues. We ourselves say Willy or Billy, Polly or Molly.

The bards have evidently confounded the god Diarmad with the mortal, as the tale of the death from the wound in the foot plainly belongs to the era of mythology. As a family or clan name it probably arose from a Druid, who adopted the name of the deity he served, or from a hero who took the name of his favourite god. Such was not an unusual custom. At Delphi, the priest who represented Bacchus was himself called by that name. The priest of Cnuphis, in Egypt, was called Se-cnuphis, the priestess of Delphi was called Pythia, from Python, and the Druid of the god Hu, whose symbol was an adder, was called Adder. In Scandinavia about B.C. 70, the hero Siggo, son of Fridulph, assumed the name of Odin, the supreme god of the Teutonic nations, and from this so-called *historical* Odin, the kings of Norway and Denmark, and the Anglo-Saxon kings derived their descent.

In Scotland, as well as in Ireland, Druidical remains abound. The Grampians were anciently called Granze-benc,* Grian's hills, and there is a hill in the parish of Fortingal, County of Perth, called Grianan hill, at the foot of which is an ancient circular building, one of the stones measuring twenty-nine feet long. This was, undoubtedly, a temple of Grian, as the sun temples were usually of a round form. In Strathspey, County of Elgin, are some Druidical remains, called Griantach or Sliabh Grianus, the heath of the Sun, who was worshipped until the time of the Romans, for it was usual with them to add the names of foreign gods to those of their own, and an altar dedicated to the Sun divinity, Apollo Gran (Apollini Granno), was found at Musselburgh.

Strathspey is called the Grant country, and the clan Grant undoubtedly derive their name from the temple of the Sun-god, and it was, probably, so understood, when

* From *ben*, a hill, the Cornish *pen*. Sleigh, which means a hill in Ireland, is used in Scotland to signify a heath.

they adopted their crest, a burning mount, which evidently refers to fire-worship.

In Gough's " Camden," (London, 1806) it is stated that in the Parish of Duthil, in Strathspey, " there is a small grove of trees held in such veneration, that nobody will cut a branch out of it."

This must have been originally a sacred grove connected with the neighbouring temple.

Baal was worshipped in the British Isles by fires called Beltan, Beltane and Beltcine, which have been kept up in some parts of England and Scotland until within the present century. The fires on the first of May were dedicated to Astarté, who had so many names that she, as Isis, was called Myrionyma, the goddess with " ten thousand names. " The Kelts of the Netherlands and Germany worshipped her as Ostara or Eoster. In Britain she appears to have been known as Ceredwin, but out of nearly one hundred of her names now before me I cannot determine by which she was worshipped in Scotland. As the consort of Tammuz she was called Baalath or Beltis, the Lady, and the Queen of Heaven and it was customary on this day, in the British Isles at least, to extinguish all the fires and rekindle them with the sacred fire obtained from the Druids. The same " Holy Fire " which is still rekindled every year by the Greek priests in the Church of the Holy Sepulchre at Jerusalem—except that in the present day the priests probably derive their " Holy Fire " from a friction match !

After the Pagan and Christian festivals were amalgamated the British Christians continued for some time to extinguish their fires on Easter Day, and to kindle them anew with fire obtained from the Roman Catholic priests *

---

* An old poet says :
" On Easter Eve the fire all is quencht in every place,
And fresh againe from out the flint is fetcht with solemne grace :
The priest doth halow this against great daungers many one,
A brande whereof doth every man with greedie minde take home

and they still, in too many cases, continue to decorate
their places of worship on that day with flowers, in the
very same manner that their pagan ancestors decorated
their altars to Astarté—ignoring entirely the words of St.
John, that, " God is a Spirit; and they that worship Him
must worship Him in spirit and in truth "—and St. Paul's,
" *Neither is worshipped by men's hands* as though he
needeth anything."

Polydore Vergil, the Pope's Legate to England in 1503,
says " Trimming of the temples with hangynges, flowers,
boughes, and garlondes, was taken of the heathen people,
which decked their idols and houses with such array ;"
and Sir Isaac Newton observes that " the Heathens were
delighted with the festivals of their gods, and unwilling
to part with those ceremonies. Therefore Gregory, Bishop
of Neo-Cæsarea, in Pontus (A.D. 264), to facilitate their
conversion, instituted annual festivals to the saints and
martyrs ; hence the keeping of Christmas with ivy,
feasting, plays and sports, came in the room of the Bacchanalia and Saturnalia ; the celebration of May-day with
flowers, in the room of the Floralia."

No scholar will venture to deny that floral decora-
tion of churches, harvest festivals and the like, were all
derived from the Pagans, through the Church of Rome.
Many of these customs and ceremonies which were given
up after the blessed Reformation, had become obsolete and
almost forgotten until revived within the last few years
by the Puseyites.

Hislop's words with regard to processions will apply
equally well to floral decorations of churches. " The very
idea is an affront to the majesty of heaven; it implies
that that God who is a Spirit sees with the eyes of flesh,

A taper great, the *Paschall* namde with musicke then they blesse,
And frankencense herein they pricke, for greater holiness ;
This burneth night and day as sign of Christ that conquerde hell,
As if so be this foolish toye suffiseth this to tell."

and may be moved by the imposing picturesqueness of
such a spectacle, just as sensuous mortals might."

Midsummer eve (June 24) was another Druidical festival which was made to correspond with St. John's Day,
and fires, now called St. John's fires, are still made in
Ireland and Britanny. In the former country they are
also called bone-fires (not bon-fires), perhaps derived from
Bann, a god of night.

The night of the first of November was also another
fire festival, afterwards called All-halloweven. The fires
made on that night were called in some parts of England
Tindels and Tinleys, and in Ayrshire Tannels.

Besides their Baal fires the Highlanders of Scotland
thought it a religious duty to walk round their fields and
flocks with burning matter in their right hands, a practice once universal throughout the country, and in every
village there was anciently a granni or gruagach* stone,
upon which libations of milk were offered on days consecrated to the Sun.

In Scandinavia Tammuz was worshipped as Odin. He
lived on wine like the classic Bacchus, or the Lamented
One, but some of his attributes appear to have been
transmitted to his sons, for the cross, as we have
already seen, was peculiar to Thor. The Scandinavian
Runic tyr, similar to our T, except that the limbs bend
downwards, was, however, sacred to Tyr, another son of
Odin, while the Runic letter Th. (somewhat resembling
our P) was sacred to Thor.

Odin's second son Balder (*Baal-zer*, the Seed of Baal),
god of the summer sun, was the Lamented one of the
North, for at his death everything was made to weep for
him. According to the belief of the ancient Scandinavians men, beasts, trees, metals, and the stones themselves
wept for him like as when the sun causes a thaw in

---

* This must have been another name of the Sun-god. Gruagach, signifies
hairy, and Apollo's long golden locks were emblematic of the sun's rays.

spring. Torches were lit up to his honour in the houses
and Baal fires were made upon the mountains, and the
people danced round them shouting and singing and
passing their children and cattle through the fires, as in
the British Isles, and like Baal's prophets of old and the
worshippers of Moloch,

These fires, called Balderbal or Balder's fires, were held
about the end of January, and were accompanied by
feasting. On the introduction of Christianity they were
replaced by the feast of Candlemas! Balder's fires were
also made on Midsummer eve, and probably also in May
and November.

In Germany fires were formerly made on the eve of
the first of May, called Walpurgis nacht.

The Egyptians on a certain night in the year as we
learn from Herodotus, burned lamps in the open air in
honour of Osiris, and in Pagan Rome, as Augustine tells
us, the temple of Vesta where the "Eternal Fire" was
kept, was the most sacred and most reverenced of all the
temples of Rome. The perpetual fire was maintained by
virgins called Vestal Virgins. In Scandinavia there were
also such virgins, priestesses of Freyja, whose duty it was
to watch the sacred fire, and in Peru, during the reign of
the Incas, there were virgins of the sun or the elect as they
were called, whose duty it also was to watch the sacred
fire. Prescott ("Conquest of Peru") was astonished to
find so close a resemblance between the institutions of
the American Indian, the ancient Roman and the modern
Roman Catholic, but does not account for it. The key,
however, is to be found in Jeremiah (li. 57) "Babylon hath
been a golden cup in the Lord's hand, that hath made
ALL THE EARTH drunken."

The Guebres of Persia. called in India Parsees, still
worship the Sun and have at Yezd (called by them the
Seat of Religion) in Persia, a Fire-Temple which they
assert had has the sacred fire in it since the days of Zoro-

aster, and Layard describes the worship of Scheick Shems by the Yezidis, of Koordistan, who once a year celebrate the festival of burning lamps to his honour.

Although I have shown that fires to Baal have been made until so lately , still it may startle some to learn that a perpetual fire, such as that of the Guebres, was kept up in Ireland until the reign of Henry the Eighth. Where Kildare now stands was formerly a sacred oak-grove of the Druids. About the end of the fifth century a Druidess was converted by St. Patrick and founded a monastery, but maintained the sacred fire in a cell where it was guarded by virgins (like the Roman vestals), often women of quality, called Inghean an Dagha, daughters of fire, and Breochuidh, or the fire-keepers, and was not extinguished until A. D. 1220, by an Archbishop of Dublin, but so firmly rooted was the veneration for this sacred fire that it was relighted in a few years and actually kept burning until the suppression of monasteries in 1539.

I trust I have now proved satisfactorily that Lights on the Altar are identical with the Babylonian Fire-worship of the Sun, (who was also adored in Job's time by wafting a kiss to him——. " If I beheld the sun when it shined . . . . And my heart hath been secretly enticed, or my mouth hath kissed my hand," Job xxxi. 16) which from the first Babylon was transmitted to the uttermost parts of the earth—for the Spaniards found Fire-worship existing in South America, where also all fires were regularly extinguished at midsummer and rekindled from the sacred fire obtained from the priests. * They believed also in a god called Wodan, whom they considered the founder of their race, and had a day called after him ex-

---

* In these days of friction matches, it may be necessary to explain that even in civilized countries, so difficult was it to light a fire with flint and steel and often *damp* tinder, that until about forty years ago people never entirely extinguished their fires at night, but covered the embers with ashes so that they might be easily raked out and rekindled.

actly as we ourselves have ; in a deluge where only one
old man and his family were saved in a bark, or on a
raft or in a cave (for the traditions of the Mexicans,
Peruvians and others differ in some slight particulars)
and revered the cross of Tammuz.

Even now the Bhuddists of Thibet burn thousands of
small candles on their shrines and present offerings of
flowers at the burial of their dead, * and the Chinese
have their annual Feast of Lanterns and burn joss-
sticks and fire-crackers before their gods.

All Heathen mythology arose in Babylon, all from corrupted traditions carried to all parts of the world by the
dispersion of races, proving most unmistakeably the truth
of the Bible narrative. They all bore away with them
faint and perverted accounts of a primitive revelation, of
the Fall of Man, of the Deluge, of the Trinity, and of the
Promise of the Redeemer, for the worship of the Serpent
always accompanied that of the Sun, who was the Serpent Sun-god, and traces of Serpent worship are to be
found everywhere, as is clearly proved by the Rev. Mr.
Shepheard ("Traditions of Eden," London, 1871), although
he has overlooked the Great Serpent in the State of Ohio,
United States of America, which winds in graceful undul-
ations for seven hundred feet, and if extended would not be
less than one thousand feet. This work of the Mound
Builders might be called extraordinary could we but for-

* Strewing the dead and their graves with flowers was a Heathen custom
reprobated by the primitive Christians, but by the time of Prudentius (4th
century) they had adopted it. It was condemned both by Ambrose and
Jerome. When that aged Christian the late Rev. Dr. Muhlenberg, of New
York (author of "I would not live alway"), died, there was added to the
notice of his death in the papers, the words "No Flowers," and I believe
that it was by his own request. Not very long since the papers contained
the account of a funeral where not only the coffin and bier, but even the
pulpit, were literally covered with flowers ; and to-day I read the following :
—"And the bouquets ! They were pitched upon the stage in barrow-loads.
Large and small, in all shapes and sizes ; wreaths big enough to hang
loosely on an elephant's brows, floral lyres large enough to fill a chair,
coronets of flowers"——. The church and the theatre ! Which will claim
the prize ?

get the Serpent-sun Temple at Avebury, in Wiltshire, England, measuring two miles in length, or the one at Snap, in Westmoreland, which, according to tradition, was originally eight miles long, or the great Serpent-sun Temple at Carnac,* in Britanny, consisting of eleven rows, which following its windings is also eight miles long.

Enormous as these Druidical erections are, for the great stone of Lochmariaker in Britanny is seventy feet in height, and the table of the great dolmen in Cornwall, which is raised upon two natural rocks, measures about 40 feet long, 20 feet wide and 16 feet thick, and weighs upwards of 700 tons ; still they are only rude, unhewn stones, and forming our opinions accordingly we probably consider the Druids as having been little better than savages, but was there not some hidden reason for their use of natural stones?

The one altar of the Jews was expressly ordained to be of unhewn stone. "And if thou wilt make me an altar of stone, thou shalt not build it of hewn stone : for if thou lift up thy tool upon it, thou hast polluted it!"

That they could execute highly finished works, is evident, not only from the sculptured stones of Scotland, but also from the few remains engraved by Montfaucon and others. It is only surprising that so few of their objects of worship have been preserved, for although overthrown at the introduction of Christianity, still it is not likely that they were all ground to powder, and as they had numerous gods, some of which, however, were very rude, their temples must have been filled with idols. Sacred woods, holy rivers and springs of water, temples, altars and images abounded. At the temple at Rottum, province of West Friesland, Netherlands, there were one hundred images of their gods, and magnificent feasts were held in their honour.

* Cairn hag—the Serpent Cairn. Snakes are still called hag-worms in the North of England.

The Britons did not dwell in huts, as one might infer
from Sharon Turner's history, for Strabo, the geographer,
who died about A.D. 20, not only mentions their exten-
sive barns, spacious buildings where they threshed their
corn, but says also that they built houses for themselves
with felled trees, and hovels for their cattle. These
differed from the log-houses of this continent, as they
were probably built of trunks of trees placed side by
side, and *standing upright*, similar to the little church
of Greenstead, co. Essex, built A.D. 1010, as a sort of
shrine only, or they may have been half timbered houses,
with the interstices filled with mortar, for lime was in
common use, as they used it for manure.

The magnificent feasts to which I have just alluded
appear to have been veritable bacchanalian orgies. Our
Pagan forefathers not only drank immoderately, but they
even drank healths in honour of the gods. Hence came
that custom among the first Christians in Germany and
the North, of drinking to the health of our Saviour, the
Apostles, and the Saints, a custom which the church was
often obliged to tolerate. We Churchmen have also our
Religious Feasts, but the Prayer Book does not tell us
in whose honour they are to be held ! In that book we
find "A Table of Feasts that are to be observed in the
Church of England." Why should the stomach enter so
largely into our devotions ?

If we strictly followed the Calendar, our lives would
be spent alternately in feasting and fasting, as there are
about ninety Feast Days, and 120 Vigils and Days of
Fasting or Abstinence.

Both festivals and fasts were common among the Heathen. As regards Lent, it arose in Babylon, and the
Yezidis, or Sun Worshippers (generally styled "Devil
Worshippers") of Koordistan, still keep a Lent of forty
days. The Egyptians observed a Lent of forty days in
honour of Osiris, and the Romans held a forty nights'

wailing for Proserpine. Humboldt tells us moreover, that three days after the vernal equinox, the Mexicans began a solemn fast of forty days in honour of the Sun.

It is true that our blessed Lord fasted forty days, but it was when he was placed in the power of Satan to be tempted by him, and may not that fast therefore have been part of the temptation? The primitive Christians did not keep a forty days' Lent, and it was only after "the mystery of iniquity" was *fully* at work that the institution of Lent was introduced into the Church by the Popes of Rome. The word "fasting" in our New Testament is an interpolation in no less than four places.* Our Saviour did not tell us to fast. When He said, "When ye fast," He was addressing the Jews who were commanded to fast by the Law." Neither did St. Paul ordain it. His words were "IN EVERYTHING by *prayer* and *supplication* with *thanksgiving*, let your requests be made known unto God,"—not a word about fasting! Is not this significant?

It is evident that the compilers of the Prayer Book could not find authority for fasting in the New Testament, as the Epistle for Ash Wednesday is taken from the Prophet Joel, who wrote eight centuries before Christ.

Durand says, that the first observation of Lent began from a superstitious, unwarrantable, and indeed profane conceit of imitating our Saviour's miraculous abstinence.

Neither feasts nor fasts are mentioned in the Prayer Book of the Reformed Episcopal Church.

But to return—Crishna, one of the gods of India, was said to have slain a serpent, and then to have died in consequence of having been shot by an arrow in the foot. He is represented as crushing the serpent's head with his foot. "Thou shalt bruise his head, and he shall bruise thy heel." Apollo slew the serpent Python; and the demi-god Achilles died from a wound in the heel, the only spot where he was vulnerable.

* Matt. xvii. 21; Mark, ix. 29; Acts, x. 30, and 1 Cor. vii. 5.

The Egyptian god Horus is frequently figured as piercing the head of a serpent with a spear, while the Scandinavian god Thor bruised the head of the Midgard serpent, and himself died from the venemous effluvia of the serpent's breath. Even in Mexico the great spirit Teotl is represented as having crushed a serpent, and one of their chief gods was called Quetzalcoatl, which signifies the feathered serpent.

Can any one for a moment doubt that the origin of these fables is a perverted history of the serpent of Paradise? Snakes are still worshipped in Asia and Africa; and in the Shangalla country they not only worship the Serpent and Sun but also, it is said, like the British Druids, cruciform trees.

It has been supposed that the legend of St. Patrick having destroyed all the serpents in Ireland is a traditional record of his having, by preaching the gospel, abolished the worship of the Serpent.

As Hislop says: " No wonder that the serpent, the Devil's grand instrument in seducing mankind, was in all the earth worshipped with such extraordinary reverence, it being laid down in the Ochtateuch of Ostanes that ' serpents were the supreme of all gods and the princes of the universe.' . . . . So deep and so strong was the hold that Satan had contrived to get of the ancient world in this character, that even when Christianity had been proclaimed to man, and the true light had shone from heaven, the very doctrine we have been considering raised its head among the professed disciples of Christ. Those who held this doctrine were called Ophiani or Ophites, that is, serpent worshippers." These heretics magnified the serpent, as having given the first knowledge of good and evil, and preferred him to Christ himself, and the sect which began in the second century lasted even into the sixth.

The Babylonians worshipped a Goddess Mother and

her child, and called her Beltis, which is equivalent to
Our Lady or Madonna, and to symbolize the doctrine of the
Trinity used the equilateral triangle just as the Romish
Church does to this day. It was one of the symbols of
Bacchus, and is also a symbol of the Hindu god Siva.
The Bull Apis, worshipped by the ancient Egyptians as
the incarnation of their great god Phtah, was required to be
black with a white triangle on his forehead. A triangle
and a fish are incised upon a stone at Stonehaven, Scotland. The double triangle is to be found in Mohammedan
countries, where it is now called the Seal of Solomon, and
in Russia most of the churches contain pictures of the
Creator, who is generally represented as an aged man,
having the triangle either in His hand or above His head.
Even the Jews, who consider that since the fall of Babylon
they have rejected all idolatrous worship, have, it is said,
a superstitious regard for the triangle,—and must I add
that it is also constantly to be met with in Protestant
churches as a symbol of that God who solemnly forbade
all similitudes for the use of religion.

"To whom then will ye liken God? or what likeness
will ye compare unto him?"

Dare any one reply—to an equilateral triangle—and
yet we place that Heathen symbol in our churches, in
carvings, in painted windows, and in Christmas decorations,
as a symbol of that Spirit who is not to be worshipped by
men's hands.

The Assyrians had a trinity composed of Anu, the
Oannes of the Greeks; Bel, sometimes worshipped as Bel
Dagon, and Ao, Hoa or Hea, the Sun; and another triad
of Shamash, the Sun; Sin, the Moon-god; and another
form of Ao, whose name is yet undecided, as in the inscriptions it is only represented by a monogram. Raw-
linson calls him Vul.

The Egyptians had several trinities. At Thebes Amen-
Ra (Amen, the Sun), Maut, the Mother, and Chons, the

D

Son. At Memphis they worshipped Phtah, Pasht, his
wife, and her child, the Sun. Month was worshipped at
Hermonthis with the Goddess Ritho, his wife, and Harphre
(Horus, the Sun) ; but the most exalted of their triads
was Osiris, Isis and Horus, who were the objects of
universal worship in all parts of Egypt. Another trinity
was Isis, the mother, Horus, her child, and Seb, father of
the gods, the worship of whom was carried to Rome; and
from this triad is derived the I. H. S., now made to bear
another signification.

In Asia, Greece and Pagan Rome, the Mother and Son
were also worshipped, and in South America they are said
to have worshipped a god whom they considered one in
three and three in one.

The Sclavs of Prussia, who were not converted until
the tenth century, had, with countless lesser gods, a
peculiar Trinity, known as Percunos, Potrimpos and Pi-
cullos, the gods of thunder, of the harvest, and of the
infernal regions.

The Brahmins of India still have their Trimurrti,
Brahma, Vishnu and Siva, and in one of their most ancient cave temples this supreme divinity is represented
with three heads on one body, under the name of "*Eko
Deva Trimurrti*," one God, three forms ; and in Japan,
Buddha is worshipped under the same form as "*San
Pao Fuh*." In Pagan Siberia there was a similar god.
The Buddhist priests had a tradition for centuries, some
say thousands of years before the Christian era, that a
virgin was to bring forth a child to bless the world ; and
can we doubt but that the Babylonians also held such a
belief, for what is Mithra but the *Mediator*, and what does
Dionusos signify but D'ion-nuso-s, *The Sin-bearer!*

The Hindoo worshippers of Vishnu bear on their foreheads the mark called Nama, consisting of
three perpendicular lines, inclining inwards at
the bottom, and crossed there by a horizon-

tal line so as to form a kind of trident;* and the favourite symbol of the Welsh bards (undoubtedly derived from the Druids) is three similar
lines, which they say stands for the name of
God.

The Hindu God Siva is called the Trident-bearer and
is represented carrying a trident. He is also called the
triple-eyed god. The priests of Buddha in Thibet also
have tridents—and this reminds me that the Greeks also
had a confused idea of the Trinity, for three of their principal deities had each a tri-form symbol : Jupiter the
three-forked lightning, besides which one of his surnames,
like Siva, was Triophthalmos, the triple-eyed; Neptune
had the trident, and Pluto the three-headed dog. The
priestess of Apollo, at Delphi, delivered her oracles from
a tripod or three-legged seat ; but it was composed of a
triple-headed serpent of brass, and the Brazen Column
still in existence at Constantinople, which is supposed to
have been brought from Delphi, is composed of three serpents.

The Pythagoreans are said to have known each other
by the number three. The Druids also had an extraordinary veneration for that number, and esteemed the
mistletoe as most sacred because not only its berries, but
its leaves also, grow in clusters of three united to one
stalk. They held, likewise, a mysterious regard for the
white clover leaf, or three-leaved clover ; and the trefoil
grass was also used in worship by the Persians. The
Greeks, too, seem to have held it in esteem, for the Rod
of Mercury was called " Rabdŏs Tripētelŏs," or The *three-
leaved* rod.

Of all the ancient nations the religion of the Egyptians
was the most profound, their sacred ceremonies the most
pompous, their feasts the most magnificent ; so that

* This seems to be also called the Tripundara, or ornament of three
stripes.

Herodotus, when he visited Egypt, was struck by their extreme devotion, and represented them as the most religious of mankind. Symbolism, however, as Le Normant says, was the very essence of the genius of the nation and their religion. The abuse of that tendency produced the grossest and most monstrous perversion of the external and popular worship in the land of Mizraim. To symbolize the attributes, the qualities, and nature of their various deities the Egyptian priests had recourse to animals, each of which was an emblem of a divine personage. The god was represented under the figure of that animal, or more frequently by the strange conjunctions peculiar to Egypt, of the head of the animal with a human body. But the inhabitants of the banks of the Nile, instinctively averse to the idolatry of other pagan nations, preferred to pay their worship to living representatives of their gods rather than to lifeless images of stone or metal, and they found these representatives in the animals chosen as emblems of the idea expressed by the conception of each god.

Hence arose that worship of sacred animals, each of whom was carefully tended during its life in the temple of the god to whom it was sacred, and after death its body was embalmed. At first these sacred animals were only the living representatives of the deities, but popular superstition soon exalted them into real gods; and finally the worship of the animals became that part of their religion to which they were most inseparably attached.

Their temples, however, were destroyed in 391; but they could not submit to part with their Goddess Mother Isis, and were determined that her worship should be restored even if under another name, in which they succeeded in the following century by introducing the worship of the Virgin Mary and her Son in the stead of Isis and Horus.

Egypt was even then suffering under the curse pronounced ages before by the prophet Ezekiel for her treachery to God's chosen people.

"And I will bring again the captivity of Egypt and will cause them to return into the land of Pathros, into the land of their habitation ; *and they shall be there a base kingdom.*

" *It shall be the basest of the kingdoms ; neither shall it exalt itself any more above the nations ; for I will diminish them that they shall no more rule over the nations.*"

Upwards of two thousand years ago was this foretold to that mother of idols, once a mistress of the nations, and has she ever had an independent sovereign since ? She is groaning under the curse still, and will continue to do so until the day foretold by Isaiah (xix, 19-25) when the Lord of Hosts shall say, " Blessed be Egypt my people, and Assyria the work of my hands, and Israel my inheritance."

Throughout Heathendom from the earliest times to the present day we find nothing but symbols and idols, from the simplest and rudest to the most elaborate works of man. Some savage tribes worship even rough stones as symbols of their gods. They have no express commandments, and will it not be better for them at the last day than for those who have received, and trifled with that Commandment ?

Even the Mahommedans, who condemn all idolatry, kiss the black stone of the Kaaba, and fill their mosques with ostrich eggs, as was anciently done in the Egyptian and Greek temples.

The mystic egg has a two-fold significance ; as the mundane egg, it had reference to the ark in which the whole human race were shut up, as the chick is enclosed in the egg before it is hatched ; and in its other aspect it was the egg out of which came Venus, who was afterwards called the Syrian Goddess, that is Astarté. Hence the egg became one of the symbols of Astarté, and the Druids wore one, set in gold, hung about their necks. It was called in Rome *orum anguinum*, serpent's egg, and the virtues ascribed to it were numerous, especially for success in law suits and interest with kings. Pliny describes it as being formed by innumerable serpents entwining themselves together and producing the egg, and adds, " I have seen that egg. It is the badge of distinction (*insigne*) which all the Druids wear, and I know that a Roman Knight of the Vocontii was put to death, by order of Claudius Cæsar, because, while pleading a cause, he had it in his bosom."

Higgins (" Celtic Druids") says of these eggs, " Instead of the natural one (which surely must have been very rare) artificial rings of stone, glass and baked clay were substituted in its room as of equal validity."

Large perforated beads of glass or vitreous paste and amber, supposed to be Druid's eggs, are occasionally found in the British Isles, and are called snake or adder stones, in Welsh, *Gleini nadroedd* (plural of *nadir*, a snake), which name, probably handed down by tradition, would seem to prove that the Britons also believed them to be made by serpents. The stones already referred to as having been found in the Netherlands may also be another form of the charm or amulet, but it appears to me that the celebrated stone of Ardvoirlich, which has been preserved in the family of Stewart of Ardvoirlich, Perthshire, from a remote period, is in all probability a true Druidical egg, except only that it is set in silver, while the Druids not only wore theirs mounted in gold but also wore gold chains, armlets or bracelets and finger-rings. This *Clach Dearg*, or Red Stone, is of pure white rock crystal, about the size and shape of a hen's egg, bound with four bands of silver of very antique workmanship. A stone similar in every respect is to be seen on the top of the Scottish sceptre preserved in the castle of Edinburgh.

The Hindus have a mystic egg as well as the Japanese, and the Chinese use dyed or painted eggs on sacred festivals.

The Romish and Greek churches adopted the mystic egg of Astarté, and consecrated it as a symbol of Christ's resurrection, and in Russia the presentation of an egg at Easter is the usual compliment among people of all ranks, high and low ; and besides the ordinary painted or dyed eggs, beautiful ones made of porcelain, sugar, chocolate, and various other materials are sold at the shops, and they frequently contain some articles of jewellery, such as a pair of diamond ear-rings, a broach, etc.

In Presbyterian Scotland, where there is neither Easter, nor Lent, nor Christmas, Astarté's day is, however known as Egg Sunday, and the school-boys vie with one another on that day, as to who can eat the most eggs.

I have seldom met with the Pasch or Easter eggs since I have resided in Toronto and supposed the custom had happily fallen into disuse ; but it has lately been revived in another form as the new-fashioned illuminated Easter cards generally bear an egg, accompanied by a religious text or motto.

Enough of Pagans and Paganism, but what shall be said for those Christians, in name at least, who worship their God with fire, and fill their churches and houses with carvings and paintings for the use of religion, with graven images and depicted images either on walls or windows,* and with similitudes of the Babylonian triangle

---

* I do not condemn all paintings in dwelling houses, for my own walls are covered, but among them there is no representation of my Divine Saviour (whose image is, I trust, in my heart), neither of saints nor of angels. I have, it is true, a Seggiola, valued both as a good copy and an heir-loom, but (and amateurs may call me a goth and skeptics a bigot) the halos, faint as they were, and the tiny cross are painted out, so that it is now no longer a Madonna, but only what Raphael really painted, an Italian peasant woman and her two babes. One little rood in a house may seem to some as trivial, but as *The Record* said lately "One rood screen and one retreat may not, perhaps, be esteemed much in a church, but one case of scarlet fever may in its progress decimate a population. It would be thought a serious thing to pass over a case of rinderpest because it was solitary."

for their God, the cross of Tammuz for their Saviour, and the dove of Juno or Astarté for their Holy Ghost !

Are not they all of Pagan origin, and is not that alone sufficient to condemn them even if we had no Commandment ? Are not they all similitudes for the use of religion and how then do they differ from idols ? Some there may be who wear the image but deny that they venerate the material cross ; but would they dare to crush that idol under their heel even as Hezekiah crushed the brazen serpent ?

We darken our churches with painted windows and thus prepare them for fire-worship or lights in the day time for ceremonial purposes, and fill the windows with images of beautiful men and lovely women which we look at with an admiration akin to worship, and blame the Romanists for carrying graven crucifixes, while we ourselves set up depicted ones.

The words of Lactantius are applicable still—" They light up candles to God as if HE lived in the dark ; and do not they deserve to pass for madmen who offer up lamps to the Author and Giver of light ?"

Three religious signs, and only three, were allotted to Christians—water, in baptism, and bread and wine in the Lord's Supper, which are not images nor likenesses of anything in heaven above, or in the earth beneath, or in the water under the earth.

" And if it seem evil unto you to serve the Lord, choose you this day whom ye will serve . . . but as for me and my house, we will serve the Lord."

APPENDIX.

Page 10, line 10. Christianity is said to have been introduced into Scotland A.D. 201; but it must have been only a very partial conversion, for Druidism, as is elsewhere shown, existed until Columba landed in Iona in 563, or more than a century after the death of the last of the Valentins.

In Wales (where a Christian church was founded about A.D. 58, by Bran ab Lyr Llediaeth, father of Caradog or Caractacus), Talliesin, who lived in the sixth century, was initiated into the mysteries of Druidism; and a Prince Hywell, who died in 1171, thus invoked his deity, "Attend thou my worship *in the mystic grove*, and whilst I adore thee maintain thy own jurisdiction."

Page 10, line 32. For "this monument," read "these monuments."

Page 29, line 29. *The Rock's* opinion of Harvest Festivals deserves to be remembered. "Far be it from us to underrate the importance of harvest-*thanksgiving*—a very different thing from harvest-*festival*—but it should always be held upon a *Sunday*, when the preacher will find his congregation infinitely more attentive to his remarks than if addressed to them on a week-day, when they know that the feasting and dancing will begin the moment the sermon is over."

Page 38, line 17. The crest of the Campbells, a boar's head, was probably adopted in allusion to Diarmad, at a period when the history of this ancestor was still fresh in every one's memory.

E

Page 40, line 21. Hollinshed (who died about 1580) says, " It is thought of some, that (King) Arthur first instituted, that the feast of Christmasse should be kept with such excesse of meats and drinks, in all kinds of inordinate banketting and revell for the space of thirteene daies together, according to the custome still used even unto this day, resembling the feasts which the Gentiles used to keepe in the honor of their drunken god Bacchus, called in Latin Bacchanalia ; wherein all kinds of beastlie lust and sensual voluptuousness was put in use. But whence so ever, or by whom so ever this insatiable gourmandise came up amongst us, suerlie a great abuse it is, to see the people at such a solemn feast, where they ought to be occupied in thanks giving to Almightie God, for the sending downe of his onlie begotten Son amongst us, to give themselves in manner wholie to gluttonic, with such maner of lewd and wanton pastimes, as though they should rather celebrate the same feasts of Baccha- nalia, and those other feasts which the Gentiles also kept, called Floralia and Priapalia, than the remembrance of Christ's nativitie, who abhoreth all maner of such ex- cesse."